DISCOVER THE TYRANNOSAURUS REX

Lucia Raatma

Our Prehistoric World:
Dinosaurs

Published in the United States of America by:

CHERRY LAKE PRESS
2395 South Huron Parkway, Suite 200, Ann Arbor, Michigan 48104
www.cherrylakepress.com

Content Adviser: Gregory M. Erickson, PhD, Dinosaur Paleontologist, Department of Biological
Science, Florida State University, Tallahassee, Florida

Reading Adviser: Marla Conn, ReadAbility, Inc.

Photo and Illustration Credits: Cover, pages 13, 18: © Warpaint/Shutterstock.com; page 5: © Science Photo
Library/Alamy; page 6: © photobank.kiev.ua/Shutterstock.com; pages 7, 11: © DM7/Shutterstock.com;
page 9: © Bob Orsillo/Dreamstime.com; page 10: © cpaulfell/Shutterstock.com; pages 12, 14–15: © Herschel
Hoffmeyer/Shutterstock.com; page 16: © Orla/Shutterstock.com; page 21: © Andrey Troitskiy/Dreamstime.com

Cherry Lake Press is an imprint of Cherry Lake Publishing Group.

Library of Congress Cataloging-in-Publication Data has been filed and is available at catalog.loc.gov.

Cherry Lake Press would like to acknowledge the work of the Partnership for 21st Century Learning, a Network
of Battelle for Kids. Please visit http://www.battelleforkids.org/networks/p21 for more information.

Printed in the United States of America

Note from publisher: Websites change regularly, and their future contents are outside of our control.
Supervise children when conducting any recommended online searches for extended learning opportunities.

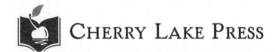

CONTENTS

WHAT WAS TYRANNOSAURUS REX?

Imagine a dinosaur that was as long as a school bus! The *Tyrannosaurus rex* was a huge, meat-eating dinosaur. It lived between 68 million and 65 million years ago. It was one of the biggest dinosaurs that ever lived. Today, all dinosaurs are extinct.

The *Tyrannosaurus rex* was a large and powerful dinosaur.

The name *Tyrannosaurus rex* means "tyrant lizard king." This dinosaur is also known as the *T. rex*. It lived in the forests of North America. It usually stayed close to rivers and swamps. Its habitat was warm and humid.

Much of the area where *T. rex* lived was wetter than it is today.

Think!

Rivers and swamps are sources of water. Why would the *T. rex* live near water sources? What other animals lived or visited there?

WHAT DID A T. REX LOOK LIKE?

The *T. rex* weighed between 5 and 8 tons (4.5 and 7.3 tonnes). It could be 42 feet (12.8 meters) long. That included its tail. The tail alone was usually 15 to 20 feet (4.6 to 6 m) long. But the *T. rex*'s arms were short. They were only about 3 feet (1 m) long.

A *T. rex*'s tail could make up as much as half of the dinosaur's total length.

Can you believe that a *T. rex*'s skull was about 5 feet (1.5 m) long? That's the height of many adult humans! In comparison, its eyes were tiny. They were only about 4 inches (10.2 centimeters) tall and wide.

Look!

Look at your own body. With an adult's help, measure how tall you are. Then measure how long your arms are. Are your arms almost as long as a *T. rex*'s? Are you almost as tall as the length of a *T. rex* skull?

A *T. rex*'s brain was small for an animal with such a large head.

The *T. rex* and *Triceratops* lived in the same area at the same time. They probably fought a lot.

The *T. rex*'s jaws were big and dangerous. They could be up to 4 feet (1.2 m) long. On those jaws were 60 thick, sharp teeth. Some teeth were very small. Others could be 6.5 inches (16.5 cm) long.

Try to picture a huge dinosaur running on its toes! That's what the *T. rex* did. Modern cats, dogs, and other animals move the same way. The *T. rex* had feet about 3 feet (1 m) long. Each foot had three large toes with sharp, eagle-like claws.

The *T. rex* had long, strong back legs.

Create!

Look at the pictures in this book. Then draw a picture of a *T. rex*. Remember how long its tail is. Show how short its arms are. Make its teeth look big and sharp!

The *T. rex* used its speed to chase down animals for food.

HOW DID A T. REX LIVE?

The *T. rex* was a fierce **predator**. Its strong legs helped it move quickly. It could run about 20 miles (32 kilometers) per hour. That's about as fast as a person on a bicycle. This dinosaur's **stride** was 12 to 15 feet (3.7 to 4.6 m) long. Its stiff tail helped provide balance for quick turns.

The *T. rex*'s jaws were among the strongest of any known carnivore.

The *T. rex* was **carnivorous**. This means it ate meat to survive. Its **prey** were mostly smaller animals, including other dinosaurs. The *T. rex* could eat up to 100 pounds (45.5 kilograms) of food in one bite! It did not nibble around the bones. Instead, it crushed the bones as it ate.

Ask Questions!

Talk to your friends and family. What are their favorite foods? Do they like mostly plants, such as fruits and vegetables? Or are they meat lovers like the *T. rex*?

Scientists have learned about the *T. rex* by studying fossils. One famous *T. rex* skeleton is known as Sue. It is on display at the Field Museum in Chicago, Illinois. It is the biggest and most complete *T. rex* skeleton that has ever been found.

Make a Guess!

How many *T. rex* fossils have scientists discovered? Research the *T. rex* and see what you can find out. Ask your teacher about the best books and websites to use.

Sue was first put on display at the Field Museum in Chicago, Illinois, in 2000.

GLOSSARY

carnivorous (kar-NIV-ur-uhss) describing animals that eat meat

extinct (ek-STINGKT) describing a type of plant or animal that has completely died out

fossils (FAH-suhlz) the preserved remains of living things from thousands or millions of years ago

habitat (HAB-uh-tat) the place and natural conditions in which a plant or animal lives

predator (PRED-uh-tur) an animal that lives by hunting other animals for food

prey (PRAY) an animal that is hunted by other animals for food

stride (STRYED) the length between an animal's feet when it walks or runs

FIND OUT MORE

Books

Braun, Dieter. *Dictionary of Dinosaurs: An Illustrated A to Z of Every Dinosaur Ever Discovered.* New York, NY: Chartwell Books, 2022.

Gray, Susan Heinrichs. *Tyrannosaurus Rex.* Mankato, MN: The Child's World, 2010.

Websites

With an adult, learn more online with these suggested searches.

National Geographic—Tyrannosaurus Rex
Get the facts about the powerful *T. rex*.

SUE at The Field Museum
Check out this huge fossil and learn about its discovery.

INDEX

ABOUT THE AUTHOR

Lucia Raatma has written dozens of books for young readers. She and her family live in the Tampa Bay area of Florida. They enjoy looking at the dinosaur fossils at the local science museum.